December 23, 2005

To My One And Only Wife Della, The Love of My Life.
With Us, It's True That Absence Makes the Heart
Grow Fonder.

For a Wonderful Wife

from your affectionate
husband. Owen

x x x x x x x

Smithsonian American Art Museum

HYLAS
PUBLISHING

www.hylaspublishing.com

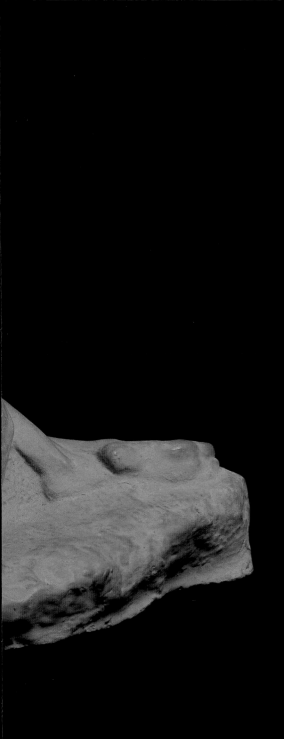

HYLAS
PUBLISHING

Hylas Publishing
Publisher: Sean Moore
Creative Director: Karen Prince
Production Consultant: Madeleine Day
Designer: Gus Yoo

First published by
Hylas Publishing
129 Main Street, Irvington,
New York 10533
www.hylaspublishing.com

First American Edition published in 2003
02 03 04 05 10 9 8 7 6 5 4 3 2 1

ISBN 1-59258-034-3

Set in Berkley and Goudy
Printed and bound in England by Butler and Tanner
Color origination by Radstock Reproductions Ltd, Midsomer
Norton

Distributed by St. Martin's Press

*On the next page you can personalize this
book by adding a photograph of your
choice, and a message.*

"The most wonderful of all things in life, I believe, is the discovery of another human being with whom one's relationship has a glowing depth, beauty, and joy as the years increase. This inner progressiveness of love between two human beings is a most marvelous thing, it cannot be found by looking for it or by passionately wishing for it.
It is a sort of Divine accident."

Sir Hugh Walpole

"Love comforteth like
sunshine after the rain."
'Venus and Adonis'
William Shakespeare
(1564-1616)

"O my Luve is like a red, red rose,
That's newly sprung in June;
O my Luve's like the melodie
That's sweetly played in tune.

As fair art thou, my bonnie lass,
So deep in luve am I;
And I will love thee still my Dear,
Til a' the seas gang dry.

Till a' the seas gang dry, my Dear,
And the rocks melt wi' the sun:
O I will love thee still my Dear,
While the sands o' life shall run.

And fare thee weel, my only Luve!
And fare the weel a while!
And I will come again, my Luve,
Tho' it were ten thousand mile!"

'A Red Red Rose'
Robert Burns (1759-1796)

"There is only
one happiness in life,
to love and be loved."
George Sand
(1804-1876)

"Women deprived of the
company of men pine,
men deprived of the
company of women
become stupid."

'Notebooks'

Anton Chekhov

(1860-1904)

"Love…

That cordial drop heaven

in our cup has thrown

To make the nauseous draught of

life go down."

'A Letter from Artemisia in the Town

to Chloe in the Country'

John Wilmot, Lord Rochester

(1647-1680)

"As you are a woman, so be lovely;

As you are lovely, so be various,

Merciful as constant, constant as various,

So be mine as I am yours forever."

'Pygmalion to Galatea'

Robert Graves (1895-1985)

"The voice that breathed o'er Eden,

That earliest wedding day,

The primal marriage blessing,

It hath not passed away."

'Holy Matrimony'

John Keble (1792-1866)

"No, there's nothing half as sweet in life

As love's young dream."

'Irish Melodies'

Thomas Moore (1779-1852)

"There may be a little trouble ahead,

But while there's moonlight and music

and love and romance,

Let's face the music and dance."

'Follow the Fleet'

Irving Berlin (1888-1989)

30

"There is a lady sweet and kind,
Was never face so pleased my mind;
I did but see her passing by,
And yet I love her till I die."

Anon.

"Who, of men, can tell

That flowers would bloom, or that green fruit would swell

To melting pulp, that fish would have bright mail,

The earth its dower of river, wood and vale,

The meadows runnels, runnels pebble-stones,

The seed its harvest, or the lute its tones,

Tones ravishment, or ravishment its sweet,

If human souls did never kiss and greet?"

'Endymion'

John Keats (1795-1821)

"Love begets love. "

Proverb

4/150

35

"How do I love thee? Let me count the ways.
I love thee to the depth and breadth and height
My soul can reach, when feeling out of sight
For the ends of Being and ideal Grace.
I love thee to the level of everyday's
Most quiet need, by sun and candlelight.
I love thee freely, as men strive for Right;
I love thee purely, as they turn from Praise.
I love thee with a passion put to use
In my old griefs, and with my childhood's faith.
I love thee with a love I seemed to lose
With my lost saints - I love thee with the breath,
Smiles, tears, of all my life! - and, if God choose,
I shall love thee better after death."

'Sonnets from the Portuguese'

Elizabeth Barrett Browning (1806-1861)

"When Love with unconfined wings

Hovers within my gates;

And my divine Althea brings

To whisper at the grates:

When I lie tangled in her hair,

And fettered to her eye;

The Gods, that wanton in the air

Know no such liberty."

'To Althea, From Prison'

Richard Lovelace (1618-1658)

"My definition of marriage…

it resembles a pair of shears,

so joined that they cannot be separated;

often moving in opposite directions,

yet always punishing anyone

who comes between them."

'Lady Holland Memoir'

Sydney Smith (1771-1845)

"Happy is the bride that the sun shines on."

Proverb

44

"All love at first, like generous wine,

Ferments and frets, until 'tis fine;

But when 'tis settled on the lee,

And from th' impurer matter free,

Becomes the richer still, the older,

And proves the pleasanter, the colder."

'Genuine Remains'

Samuel Butler (1612-1680)

"Give me a thousand kisses, then a hundred,
then another thousand, then a second hundred,
then yet another thousand, then a hundred."

'Carmina'

Catullus (84-54 BC)

48

"My heart was not in me
but with you,
and now, even more,
if it is not with you
it is nowhere."

Heloise (1098-1164)

"Love guards the roses of thy lips

And flies about them like a bee;

If I approach he forward skips,

And if I kiss he stingeth me.

Love in thine eyes doth build his bower,

And sleeps within their pretty shine;

And if I look the boy will lour,

And from their orbs shoot shafts divine."

'Love Guards the Roses of Thy Lips'

Thomas Lodge (1558-1625)

OCTOBER

W. C. RICE. JR. 1903

"What thou art is mine;

Our state cannot be severed, we are one,

One flesh; to lose thee were to lose my self."

'Paradise Lost'

John Milton (1608-1674)

"Women are really much nicer than men:

No wonder we like them."

'A Bookshop Idyll'

Kingsley Amis (1922-1995)

"I knew it was love, and I felt it was glory."

'Stanzas Written on the Road

Between Florence and Pisa,

November 1821'

Lord Byron (1788-1824)

"Oh, what a dear ravishing thing

is the beginning of an Amour!"

'Emperor of the Moon'

Aphra Behn (1640-1689)

"Chains do not hold
a marriage together.
It is threads,
hundreds of tiny threads
which sew people together
through the years."
Simone Signoret (1921-1985)

"But true love is a durable fire,

In the mind ever burning,

Never sick, never old, never dead,

From itself never turning."

'Walsinghame'

Walter Raleigh (1552-1618)

"Marriages are made in heaven."

Proverb

ClaudeBuck

65

"Love conquers all things:

let us too give in to love."

Virgil (70-19 BC)

25 26 27 28 29

30  31  32  33

Picture Credits

All images are from The Smithsonian American Art Museum

1. *Chicago Interior,* ca. 1934, J. Theodore Johnson **2.** *The Mirror,* ca. 1910, Robert Reid **3.** *Couple Embracing,* Laura Dreyfus Barney **4.** *Dublin Pond,* 1894, Abbott Handerson Thayer **5.** *Tanagra (The Builders, New York),* 1918, Childe Hassam **6.** *Cape Cod Morning 1950,* Edward Hopper **7.** *Roses Still Life,* ca. 1842-1848, Robert S. Duncanson **8.** *August Breakfast/Maine,* 1997, © Carolyn Brady **9.** *Artists on WPA,* 1935, Moses Soyer **10.** *Fan,* 1775-1800, Unidentified **11.** *Young Girl in Purple,* 1930, Alexandre Hogue **12.** *The Bride, ca.* 1907, Gari Melchers **13.** *Wedding Cake Basket,* 1986, Mary Adams **14.** *Street Musicians,* ca. 1940, William H. Johnson **15.** *Marechal Niel Roses,* 1919, Childe Hassam **16.** *Somnolence,* Frank Edwin Scott **17.** *Love,* 1973, Robert Indiana **18.** *The Violet Kimono,* ca. 1910, Robert Reid **19.** *The Perfume of Roses,* 1902, Charles C. Curran **20.** *One Day in June,* ca. 1880-1885, William Thomas Smedley **21.** *A Bride,* ca. 1895, Abbott Handerson Thayer **22.** *Her Leisure Hour,* ca. 1925, Irving R. Wiles **23.** *(The Seven Ages of Man, portfolio) (Embrace),* 1918, Rockwell Kent **24.** *Roses,* ca. 1896, Abbott Handerson Thayer **25.** *The Viking's Daughter,* 1887, Frederick Stuart Church **26.** *October* (cover illustration for Harper's magazine), 1903, William Clarke Rice **27.** *June,* ca. 1911, John White Alexander **28.** *Woman Sowing,* Robert Gwathmey **29.** *Easter Greetings,* ca. 1895, Walter Shirlaw **30.** *Bargain Hunters,* 1940, Kenneth Hayes Miller **31.** *The Spinet,* ca. 1902, Thomas Wilmer Dewing **32.** *Cowboy Dance,* (Mural Study, Anson, Texas Post Office) 1941, Jenne Magafan

Acknowledgments: Hylas Publishing would like to thank Robert Johnston, Smithsonian American Art Museum, Tricia Wright for proofreading, and Ellen Nanney, Smithsonian Institution, for co-ordinating the project.